CHRISTMAS JOKES

To all those who received
a book from me
as a Christmas present...
**They are due back at the
library today.**

Who is never hungry
at Christmas?
**The turkey - he's
always stuffed!**

What is the difference between the Christmas alphabet and the ordinary alphabet? **The Christmas alphabet has NO EL.**

✳ ✳ ✳ ✳ ✳

How does Jack Frost get to work?
By icicles

Why didn't the Christmas Cake go to the dance?
He had his raisins...

What did Dracula say at the Christmas party?
Fancy a bite?

What did the strawberry
say on December 25th?
Berry Christmas!

What do you get if you cross
a cat with Santa
Santa Claws!

 ✳ **CHRISTMAS JOKES** ✳

Did you hear about
Dracula's Christmas party?
It was a scream!

✳ ✳ ✳ ✳ ✳

How does NASA organize
their Christmas party?
They planet.

Why was the snowman embarrassed at the grocery store?
He got caught picking his nose!

What does Tarzan
sing at Christmas?
Jungle Bells

✳ ✳ ✳ ✳ ✳

Why did it rain on
Christmas Eve?
**Because of Santa and
his Raindeer.**

What's the best thing to put into a Christmas cake?
Your teeth!

I carry a stone around to throw at anyone I hear singing Christmas songs before Thanksgiving.
I call it my Jingle Bell Rock

✻ ✻ ✻ ✻ ✻

What's Scrooge's favorite Christmas game?
Mean-opoly.

What does Santa suffer from if he gets stuck in a chimney?
Santa Claustrophobia!

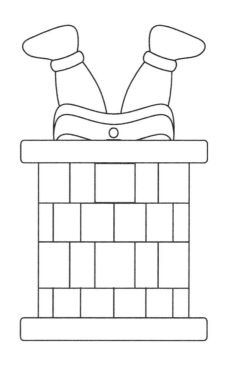

Why do we have a Thanksgiving holiday? Student: **"So we know when to start Christmas shopping!"**

✳ ✳ ✳ ✳ ✳

If you love Christmas so much, why don't you merry it?

✳ CHRISTMAS JOKES ✳

FUN FACT: Bears hibernate in the winter just to get away from Christmas music...

How did Darth Vader know what Luke got him for Christmas?
He felt his presents.

What did the ghosts say to Santa Claus?
We'll have a boo Christmas without you.

What did the snowman
say when he got coal for
Christmas?
I can see!

Why couldn't the skeleton go to the Christmas Party?
He had no body to go with!

*   *   *   *   *

How do sheep in Mexico say Merry Christmas?
Fleece Navidad!

What's fat and jolly and
runs on eight wheels?
Santa on roller skates!

Coffee asked "Why do I always get coal in my stocking."
Santa: Because your on the Not Tea list.

✳ ✳ ✳ ✳ ✳

What does Santa teach his elves?
The Elfabet!

People who complain that my Christmas gifts are "stupid" and "thoughtless" clearly have no idea how hard it is to wrap a pineapple.

Can you name all of
Santa's reindeers?
No, they already have
names.

✳ ✳ ✳ ✳ ✳

Why does everyone start to
fight the day after Christmas?
Because it's Boxing Day!

Where does Santa store his money?
In a snowbank.

What do you call a kid who doesn't believe in Santa?
A rebel without a Claus.

✳ ✳ ✳ ✳ ✳

Santa is the ultimate hipster. Works one day a year and spends the rest of the year judging you.

Why do mummies like Christmas so much?
Because of all the wrapping!

What did Santa Claus say
when Mrs. Claus asked him
about the weather?
It's rain, dear!

✳ ✳ ✳ ✳ ✳

How do you know that
Santa is a man?
**No woman wears the
same attire every year.**

What's white, red and blue at Christmas time?
A sad candy cane!

What did the cow get for Christmas?
A COWculator.

✳ ✳ ✳ ✳ ✳

Which of Santa's reindeers has bad manners?
Rude-olph!

Where did Santa Claus go for vacation?
Santa Cruz.

What's red and white, red and white, red and white?
Santa Claus rolling down the hill.

✳ ✳ ✳ ✳ ✳

How much did Santa pay for his sleigh?
Nothing, it was on the house!

What's white and red and goes up and down and up and down?
Santa Claus in an elevator!

* CHRISTMAS JOKE BOOK *

What did the Christmas tree
say to the ornament?
**"Aren't you tired of hanging
around?"**

Why did Sponge Bob have
a great Christmas?
**Because he kissed Krabby
Patty.**

How long should a reindeer's legs be? **Just long enough to reach the ground!**

What is a snowman's favorite food? **Ice Krispy treats.**

✳ CHRISTMAS JOKE BOOK ✳

What do they sing under the ocean during the winter?
Christmas Corals!

✳　✳　✳　✳　✳

What falls in the winter and never gets hurt?
Snow!

✳　CHRISTMAS JOKES　✳

How do you know Santa is good at karate?
Because he has a black belt!

✳ ✳ ✳ ✳ ✳

What's the best thing to give your parents for Christmas?
A list of everything you want!

What do snowmen eat for breakfast?
Snowflakes!

✳   ✳   ✳   ✳   ✳

What do you call Santa when he stops moving?
Santa Pause!

Why there are only
snowmen and not
snowwomen?
**Because only men would
stand out in snow without a
coat.**

✳   ✳   ✳   ✳   ✳

What type of diet did the
snowman go on?
The Meltdown Diet.

Why do Rappers like Christmas so much?
Because of all the wrapping!

✳ ✳ ✳ ✳ ✳

Who delivers Christmas presents to dogs?
Santa Paws.

What did the snowflake say
to the road?
Let's stick together.

✳ ✳ ✳ ✳ ✳

When does Christmas
come before Thanksgiving?
In the dictionary.

What do you call a
Christmas duck?
A Christmas quacker!

＊ ＊ ＊ ＊ ＊

What do you call a
snowman in the summer?
A puddle!

What do snowmen wear on their heads?
Ice caps!

✳　✳　✳　✳　✳

Why are Christmas trees such bad knitters?
They always drop their needles.

Where do snowmen
go to dance?
The snowball.

✳ ✳ ✳ ✳ ✳

What do you call an old
snowman?
Water.

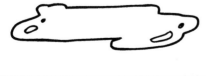

What two countries should the chef use when he's making Christmas dinner?
Turkey and Greece.

Why did the snowman go to the doctor?
He was feeling chilled!

What do you get when you cross a snowman with a vampire?
Frostbite.

* * * * *

What's white and goes up?
A confused snowflake!

How do snowmen get around?
On icycles!

✳ ✳ ✳ ✳ ✳

What did one snowman say to the other?
It all smells like carrots to me.

Why didn't the wig get any presents on Christmas?
Because it was very knotty.

✳ ✳ ✳ ✳ ✳

Why did the snowman pick through a bag of carrots?
Because he was picking his nose.

How do you scare a
snowman?
You get a hairdryer!

✳　✳　✳　✳　✳

What do Snowmen call
their offspring?
Chill-dren.

✳ CHRISTMAS JOKE BOOK ✳

What says, "Now you see me, now you don't, now you see me, now you don't?"
A snowman on a cross walk!

✳ ✳ ✳ ✳ ✳

What did the snowman order at the fast food restaurant?
An ice burger with chili sauce.

✳ CHRISTMAS JOKES ✳

What did the snowman ask
the other snowman?
Do you smell carrots?

✳ ✳ ✳ ✳ ✳

Did you hear about the
cracker's Christmas party?
It was a BANG!

GENERAL JOKES

I've always wanted a job cleaning mirrors...
It's just something I can see myself doing.

I'd like to tell you a joke about paper... but it's tearable.

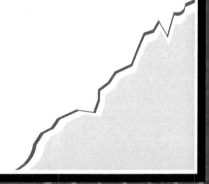

What did the bunny want to do when he grew up?
Join the Hare Force.

Maybe if I took my problems to the gym they'd work themselves out.

Why can you not hear a pterodactyl going to the bathroom?
Because the 'P' is silent.

Why did the scarecrow win the Nobel peace prize? **Because he was outstanding in his field!**

I get the whole 3 meals a day thing but I'm confused about how many at night?

If your partner asks, "Do you love your phone more than you love me?" **Lie.**

How many optimists does it take to change a light bulb?
Who says it's dark?

What has eyes but can't see, has legs but can't walk, and has wings but can't fly?
A dead bird.

Why can't a bike stand on its own ?
Because it's two tired.

Did you hear about the
restaurant on Mars?
....**The food was great, but
there was no atmosphere.**

Why did the left shoe
marry the right?
**Because they were
"sole"-mates**

Where won't you find a
dog shopping?
At the flea market!

What did the happy slice
of cheese say to the sad
slice of cheese?
**"Aw, it will be okay!
Everything is GOUDA!"**

What is Dracula's favorite
fruit?
A Blood Orange.

What did one hair say to the other?
It takes two to tangle!

What did one firefly say to the other?
You glow, girl!

Where do pencils come from?
Pennsylvania.

What's a ballerina's
favorite type of bread?
A bun.

Who did the monster ask
to kiss his boo-boos after
he fell?
His mummy.

What do you get when you
cross a fish and an
elephant?
Swimming trunks!

What do you call a bunny
with fleas?
Bugs Bunny.

What kind of shoes do
mice like?
Squeakers!

What do you get when you
put jeans in the
microwave?
Four hotpockets.

Why do cowboys ride horses?
Because they're too heavy to carry.

What is shark's favourite food?
Fish and ships.

What do you get when you cross a lamb and a rocket?
A space sheep!

Why does a stork stand on one leg?
Because it would fall over if it lifted the other one!

What is a computer's favorite snack?
Computer chips!

What kind of dog does a vampire have?
A bloodhound.

Why was the baseball
game so hot?
Because all the fans left!

What do you call a
boomerang that won't
come back?
A stick.

What do cats wear to bed?
Paw-jamas.

Why is it hard for a ghost
to tell a lie?
**Because you can see right
through him.**

How do you know a
snowman crawled into bed
with you?
**You wake up wet and
there's a carrot on your
pillow!**

What did one tooth say to the other tooth?
The dentist is taking me out tonight.

What is a skeleton's favourite instrument?
The trombone.

Why can't you take a test in the zoo?
There are too many cheetahs!

What do witches order at hotels?
Broom service.

What is the capital of Greece?
G.

What is a snowman's favorite drink?
An ice-cappuccino!

Why was Dracula put in jail?
He tried to rob a blood bank.

What has 6 legs, 4 eyes, 4 ears, 2 noses, 2 mouths and 2 heads?
A man sitting on a horse.

What time is it when an elephant sits on your fence?
Time to get a new fence.

What is cow's favourite
movie?
Moo-lan.

What cat likes living in
water?
An octoPUSS!

What sport do hairdressers
love the most?
CURLING!

Where do fish keep their money?
In the riverbank.

Why doesn't the elephant use the computer?
Because it is afraid of the mouse!

Where do planets and stars study?
UNIVERSity!

What is the cleanest
reindeer called?
Comet.

How do you know when
the moon has enough to
eat?
When it's full.

What do you call the king
of vegetables?
Elvis Parsley.

What animal carries an umbrella around?
A reindeer!

Where do sheep go on vacation?
The Baaa-hamas.

What's black and white over and over again?
A penguin rolling down a hill.

What kind of vegetable
is angry?
A steamed carrot!

How do you make cool
music?
**Put your CD's in the
fridge.**

What did the peanut say
to the walnut?
Nothing. Nuts can't talk.

What can you catch but
never throw?
A cold.

What is Dracula's
favorite fruit?
Neck-tarines.

What is a reindeer's
favorite instrument?
Horns!

If the chicken crossed the road to get to the other side, how did the frog cross the road?
He tied himself to the chicken.

What do you call a dinosaur with a big vocabulary?
A theSAURUS!

Why did the rope go to the doctor?
It had a knot in its stomach.

Why are skeletons afraid of dogs?
Because dogs love bones!

Why did the student bring scissors to class?
He wanted to cut class!

What do ghosts wear on their feet?
BOOts.

What's a vampire's favourite part of the guitar?
The neck.

What is the difference between a worn out runner and a worn out vet?
One's dog tired and the other is tired of dogs.

What do ghosts serve for dessert?
Ice SCREAM and BOOberries!

What do you get when
you cross a parrot and a
caterpillar?
A walkie talkie.

Why was the dog sitting
next to the fire?
He was a hotdog!

What is a duck's favorite
dance?
The quackstep!

What's a librarian's favorite type of bait when fishing?
Bookworms.

Why were bikes suspended from school?
They spoke too much.

What has the fur of a cat, the whiskers of a cat, ears of a car, a tail of a cat, but is not a cat?
A kitten.

Where do pencils go for vacation?
Pencil-vania.

How did the telephone propose to his girlfriend?
It gave her a ring!

What has words but never speaks?
A book.

JOKES FOR ADULTS

Why is getting Christmas presents for your kids just like a day at the office? **You do all the work and the fat guy in the suit gets all the credit.**

At work I noticed the computer department have started putting Christmas decorations up IT's beginning to look a lot like Christmas.

I'm like the fruit cake of my family. Nobody likes me but I show up every Christmas anyway.

It's Christmas Eve, not Christmas and Steve. Get out of here Steve.

Mum Can I have a dog
for Christmas?
**No you can have turkey
like everyone else!**

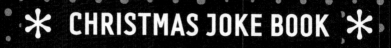

Why is Santa always jolly?
Because he knows where all the naughty girls live.

Sick of all these Santa apologists.
A HOME INVASION IS A HOME INVASION.

What are you getting this Christmas? asked my friend.
I said, "Fatter."

What did Adam say to Eve on the day before Christmas?
It's Christmas, Eve.

I'm not sure who's more drunk, me or the guy wrapped in Christmas lights standing in the mirror.

Doctor Doctor I keep thinking I'm a Christmas bell!
Just take these pills - and if they don't work give me a ring!

Doctor Doctor I'm scared of Santa Claus
Doctor: You're suffering from Claus-trophobia.

Who delivers presents to baby sharks at Christmas?
Santa Jaws!

Boy: I want a brother for Christmas.
Santa: Send me your mother.

Can I have your picture, So Santa Claus knows exactly what to give me this CHRISTMAS.

For Christmas I asked for the best looking person around.

The next morning I woke up in a box.

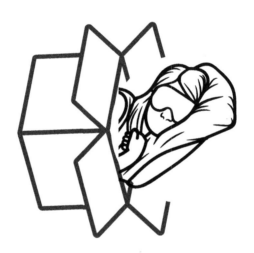

The only reason kids like Christmas is because they're not the ones buying all the presents.

'I've been a very naughty girl!' she said, licking her lips,
'I need to be punished ...'
So he invited his mother to stay for Christmas.

What's the difference....
Between my girlfriend and Santa?
Some people actually believe Santa exist.

Who does Santa think he is, judging me?
I might be naughty, but he's fat.

What nationality is Santa Claus?
North Polish.

Why do children cry
when they find out
Santa isn't real?
**They figured out who
has been drinking their
milk and eating the
cookies!**

The worst thing about finding out Santa isn't real is that you know who to blame for all the terrible presents.

Why do pens get sent to prison?
To do long sentences!

Santa should promote clean energy this year. Instead of a lump of coal he should give a can of biofuel to the bad kids.

What did Cinderella say when her photos didn't arrive on time?
One day my prints will come.

A skeleton walks into a bar, sits down and says **"I'll have a beer and a mop".**

A neutron walks into a bar... ...and asks "how much for a drink?" The bartender replies "**For you, no charge.**"

If I had a dozen muffins and Carlos took 13 away from me, what do I have now?
A math problem.

What do you call a bicycle with no seat?
A real pain in the ass.

Freak people out in public restrooms by saying "come in" when they knock on the stall door.

What do Greek soccer players wear?
Soccer tee's.

I don't pretend to be anything I'm not.. Except for sober I've pretended to be sober a few times.

Boy, do I love soccer?
It's the only sport where
the fans are tougher then
the players.

I'm against cloning. It's
Adam and Eve, not Adam
and Adam and Adam and
Adam.

Who would kick the rock's ass in a fight?
Paper.

What is love? The energy of life. What is marriage?
The energy bill ...

There's a reason why "sober" and "so bored" sound almost exactly the same.

If you want your dreams to be as fascinating to other people as they are to you, don't mention it's a dream until the end of the story.

What's the difference between an enzyme and a hormone?
You can't hear an enzyme.

Printed in Great Britain
by Amazon

14247913R00059